C.P.V

Make the perfect advertising team

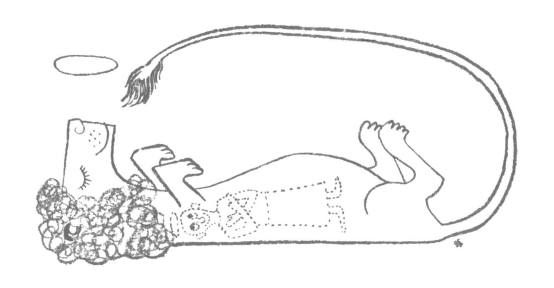

Are you full of good ideas?

Do come and see us

Colman, Prentis and Varley Limited

34 Grosvenor Street, London, W.1.

RUTH ARTMONSKY

THE BEST ADVERTISING COURSE IN TOWN

 THE HALCYON DAYS OF
COLMAN, PRENTIS & VARLEY

'...A YEAR WITH VARLEY IS THE BEST
POST-GRADUATE COURSE IN ADVERTISING
YOU'LL EVER GET' JOHN HOBSON

ACKNOWLEDGEMENTS

My thanks go to Ralph Montagu and Martha Varley whose
enthusiasm and generosity speeded my research; and my gratitude to
past employees of CPV and their relatives – Margaret Edwards, Geof
Haskins, Roger Pemberton, Judy Peppitt, John Ross, David Holmes,
Liz Smith and Stephen Spicer. As usual the book owes much to the
knowledge and creativity of my regular designer Brian Webb, and to
Dot Thompson and Dan Smith for their considerable labours.

The cover image is reproduced from *CPViana,* the CPV in-house
journal. the endpapers and frontispiece from various CPV self-
advertisements, from *ARK*, the Royal College of Art magazine, and
opposite, from the cover of the 21st birthday edition of *CPViana*, 1955.

Published by Artmonsky Arts
Flat 1, 27 Henrietta Street
London WC2E 8NA
Telephone 020 7240 8774
Email artmonskyruth@gmail.com

ISBN 978-0-9573875-9-1
All Rights Reserved
Copyright 2015 Ruth Artmonsky
Designed by Webb & Webb Design
Printed by Northend Creative Print Solutions

CONTENTS

"C.P.V flourish because their roots are in the right place..."

INTRODUCTION

Researching for a book on Crawford's, one of the major British advertising agencies in the inter-war years, was relatively easy. Crawford's agency was at the forefront of introducing modernism to advertising art and, consequently, being continuously featured in the commercial art and graphic design press; Crawford, himself, was no shy violet, but put himself about – was on a vast number of committees, advised the government on a number of issues, spoke at meetings and festivities throughout the land, was frequently being photographed by the press, and occasionally put pen to paper.

The experience of completing the book was so pleasant that I turned next to reviving the significance of another agency, and it seemed natural to take up Colman, Prentis & Varley (CPV), as the three men so named had all worked at Crawford's and had decided to break free to see what they could achieve for themselves.
I soon became aware that the task was of a rather different nature – Prentis was dead within a dozen years of the establishment of the agency, Colman, who was a shadow of a personality at Crawfords, faded into the wallpaper at CPV, and although Varley was around for much of the life of the agency, was on His Majesty's Service during WWII, and on his return spent much of his time on the road, in the air or on a ship, developing the agency overseas. And, in spite of owning an outsize Rolls Royce, Varley seems to have been in some ways a modest man, certainly in comparison with Crawford.

Opposite: André François, illustration for CPV self advertisement from ARK magazine

He did not devote much time to philosophising on the role of advertising in the modern world, either on the rostrum or on the page, nor was he as prominent in dealing with government or other influential organisations.

A further challenge to compiling the book, was the transitory nature of CPV staff. Although some sterling souls survived the course, there was a constant coming and going and even returning of staff, and, what seems to have been not infrequent, a changing of the names of staff positions, so it is not always easy to understand who was managing whom; this in comparison to Crawford's mainstays – Ashley Havinden and the two formidable Sangster sisters, who were by his side throughout. David Holmes, for example, a CPV artist, claims the record of having come and gone three times!

Additionally there was the problem that there is no comprehensive CPV archive to draw on. The History of Advertising Trust holds several guard books and similar material, mainly images, and it became necessary to fall back on the sentimental relics of ephemera kept by past employees, along with their memories and anecdotes, which tended to be quite strong in colour but altogether less clear in chronology. Putting the book together has been a matter of collecting a miscellany of thin threads and weaving them together into a patchy tapestry with some rather ragged parts and some holes. But it has been worth doing if only to remind people of one of the leading British advertising agencies in its halcyon days in the 1950s and 60s.

GETTING ESTABLISHED

Opposite: Terence Prentis, Hans Schleger and Tony Page at Crawford's, c1930.

Above: 34 Grosvenor Street, illustration by Evadné Rowan, drawn in 1955 for *CPViana*.

In 1934, a young married couple, Terence and Betty Prentis, both commercial artists, decided to set up a business together – Terence was about thirty, Betty somewhat younger. Terence had studied art at the Byam Shaw & Vicat Cole School of Art and at the Royal Academy Schools, and had already made something of a name for himself when working in Germany and in London. In Germany, he had worked in the Berlin office of Crawford's advertising agency and is occasionally referred to as being its art director, but his youth and inexperience at the time would have likely placed him junior to Ashley Havinden and Hans Schleger.

Commercial Art, in 1927, featured a short illustrated article on Prentis' work, which predicted 'he should go a very long way towards success', and declared him 'a poster artist who understands fully the function of a poster, and who most successfully practices his art'. He would have been about twenty four at the time!

'Mr Prentis works in simple designs, strong colour contrasts and he masses colour. No clutter of detail, no spotting of colours for Terence Prentis. His strongest effects are won by an economy of means. And in his work there is not only design but aptness of design.'

Prentis was, in fact, becoming a versatile designer, applying his talents not only to posters and advertisements, but to rugs, toys, book

Terence Prentis, cover illustration for
The Chapbook, Number 37, May 1923

jackets and illustration as well. In the early 1920s, he contributed cover illustrations and editorial to Harold Monro's *Chapbook* magazine.

When he was back in Crawford's London office Prentis' views on art and advertising were being sought – in 1929 by the distinguished German graphic design magazine GBG (*Gebrauchsgraphik*) and, in 1931, by *Art & Industry*. For the latter he wrote something on poster design –

> 'A poster. If it is to be of any service must be original and dramatic. It must create a mood or atmosphere which can be defined as providing a particular personality for the product. It must put forward a message which in itself is vibrant and dramatic, and the message must be told upon a note of urgency.'

Prentis had had a little experience of freelance work before joining Crawford's so would have had some awareness of the possible insecurity of breaking away to work independently.

Of Betty, little is recorded, either of her training or early work experience, although she did, later on, make a brief mention that at one time she had designed dresses. What is documented is that both she and Terence, whilst at Crawford's, worked on the Jaeger account and it would seem that on the strength of suspecting that they would be able to carry this account with them, they decided to break away. A possible reason for Terence leaving Crawford's may have been that he felt his career progress to be blocked by Ashley Havinden, who was, by the early 1930s, firmly entrenched as a director.

That things did not quite turn out the way the Prentises expected, is possibly evidenced by the fact that, within a year, they had been joined by Robert Colman and Arthur Varley, both ex-colleagues at

Terence Prentis, rhyme sheet design for *The Song of the Wooden Soldiers*, 1926 (left) and Swan & Edgar poster, 1927 (right)

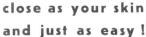

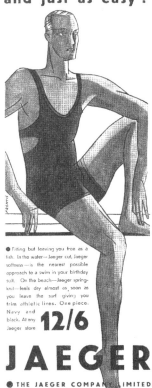

close as your skin and just as easy !

● Fitting but leaving you free as a fish. In the water—Jaeger cut, Jaeger softness—is the nearest possible approach to a swim in your birthday suit. On the beach—Jaeger spring-knit—feels dry almost as soon as you leave the surf giving you trim athletic lines. One piece. Navy and black. At any Jaeger store **12/6**

JAEGER

● THE JAEGER COMPANY LIMITED
352-54 OXFORD STREET LONDON W.1

Advertisements for Jaeger, by Terence Prentis, *Punch*, July 1930 (above) and Betty Prentis, 1931 (right), produced by W.S. Crawford Limited.

● COATS FROM benign and natural camels — at the JAEGER fashion floor, Oxford Street

JAEGER

Travels of elysian elegance START at the JAEGER fashion floor, OXFORD STREET

JAEGER

Only the lambiest lambs supply the JAEGER Fashion Floor, Oxford St.

JAEGER

For really spirit-lifting GARMENTS JAEGER fashion floor, OXFORD ST.

JAEGER

All the most amusing people shop on The JAEGER Fashion Floor, Oxford St.

JAEGER

Crawford's, the new collaboration bearing all their names – Colman, Prentis & Varley (CPV) – presumably in alphabetical order rather than by relative age, assets or ability, albeit, it was thought that Betty had a considerable financial investment in the enterprise.

Robert (Bob) Colman is a somewhat shadowy figure, barely referred to either in the records of Crawford's or of CPV. It is generally accepted that he was a member of the Colman Mustard family of Norwich. As the Prentises were to bring Jaeger into CPV, so Colman brought in Norvic Shoes, another Norwich based company. Much later on, after WWII, CPV took on Lesley Court from Reckitt & Colman to run its export side; and when Colman was away serving in the war another Colman, initialled C, acted as Chairman of CPV. These various threads seem to confirm the family connection. However, Colman's contribution to Crawford's, or to CPV, is not at all clear, although the odd reference to his having responsibility for printing and production suggests he was an administrator rather than an entrepreneur or on the creative side of the business. Nevertheless although Bob appears to have had a backroom role, he was to become a Director and to have stayed with the agency for the rest of his working life.

With Terence clearly marked out as Art Director of the new concern, it remained to Varley (Arthur Noel Claude) to take the entrepreneurial role, so essential at the start up of a company. Varley, the son of a Yorkshire parson, was educated at Winchester and had gained an exhibition scholarship to read history at Worcester College, Oxford University. Although clever, his interests lay as much on the sports field as in academia, for he was something of an athlete and rowed for his college. Nevertheless he gained a solid second class degree, which would have made difficult an academic career and left possible employment ill-defined.

In Step with Spring

New freshness in the air, an added zest to life — time for new clothes *and* new shoes to face the gay mood of Spring. What better choice for your footwear than Norvic and Mascot ! These beautifully styled British shoes combine grace of line with comfort to an exceptional degree. Try a pair to-morrow…you won't be able to resist the casual way your foot slips easily and gently into their flattering shapes.

MASCOT Easiform 8187 in Black, Brown, Hazel or Blue Glacé Kid. 21/9

MASCOT 1103SM in Black, Brown, Blue or Green Glacé Calf - - 16/9

NORVIC and MASCOT

MEN'S NORVIC AND MASCOT ARE MADE AT NORTHAMPTON

★ *Brochure of Spring styles and the name of your nearest agent free on request from*
THE NORVIC SHOE CO. LTD., NORWICH

Advertisement for Norwich based Norvic Shoe Company, 1930s

Story has it that whilst Varley had taken a temporary position in Switzerland, tutoring the sick son of a businessman, his path crossed with that of Bill Crawford, who was a friend of Varley's pupil's parents. Crawford is said to have been so immediately impressed with this bright young man that he offered him a job. At first Varley was reluctant to take up the offer as he hadn't a very positive image of the advertising profession, but, in pressing need of an income, he finally agreed. He was to start as a copywriter but seems soon to have moved to being an account executive. Elizabeth Montagu, who was to marry Varley much later on, recorded in her memoirs, that before long he was to be entrusted with major accounts and found himself travelling over Europe to service these. He was to bring at least two of these accounts with him to CPV – Elizabeth Arden and Horrockses. He was, in fact, to find advertising very much to his liking.

Varley later wrote of the ambitions of this youthful band –

'When we began we weren't concerned with doing art-rate advertising or with telling industrialists how to run their business. Nor, quite honestly, did we want to make a fortune. We were interested solely in the creation of extremely good advertisements.'

That the early motivation was not entirely so altruistic is evidenced by the fact that from the start CPV appears to have been determined to be a 'classy' agency. By 1930 there were some three hundred and fifty general advertising agencies in London, the majority of these either in the City or in the Holborn/Strand area – J. Walter Thompson, for example, was in the Aldwych, Benson's in Kingsway and the London Press Exchange in St. Martin's Lane. Whereas Crawford's was in the most modernist of buildings, designed by Frederick Etchells, in High Holborn, Varley and his partners chose an 18th century building in

FASHION'S FAVOURITE FABRICS

come to town

Go to your favourite shop and examine Horrockses wonderful materials — for your dresses, for your lingerie, for your children. See their enchanting new designs, feel their exquisite texture. Think what charming things you could make with these wonderfully inexpensive materials. There is a Horrockses fabric for every need — and for every pocket.

HORROCKSES IN THE HOME

Sheets, pillow-cases, bedspreads and towels — in the most fashionable styles. Remember, Horrockses fabrics have been famous for every household purpose for over a hundred years.

HORROCKSES

Advertisements for Horrockses, Crewsdon & Co., drawn by Hans Schleger, c1935 (left) and for Jaeger (detail above) designed by Betty Prentis, produced by W.S. Crawford Limited, 1932

Mayfair, number 34 Grosvenor Street (having been for a short time in Old Burlington Street where a CPV financial adviser had his office at the time). CPV was to remain at number 34 throughout most of its existence, albeit as it grew its arty section and others were to be deposited in an overspill at number 43.

David Smith, a postwar creative director at CPV penned a humorous description of number 34 –

'Within we've rather gone to town, your grace,
And made the hall a light and lofty place
With gently rising treads to every stair
And balustrade of ironwork, light as air;
Two doorways in the proper classic style,
And plast'ring worthy of a noble pile.'

34 Grosvenor Street,
London, interior and
exterior, 1970s

Joyce Booth, a one-time art director, recalled the fun of being
in the centre of things – the Oxford Street shops and the Bond
Street galleries; and then there was the excitement of seeing the
comings and goings at Claridges, with the likes of King Hussein of
Jordan, Barbara Cartland, David Niven, and Edith Sitwell, arriving
and departing.

Margaret Edwards, a young artist who worked closely with the art
director Ruth Gill, tells of how the hierarchy of CPV was spread
appropriately over the floors at number 34, the management on
the ground floor, the artistic rabble in the attics; when the film and
television section was formed it was placed in the basement. In the
post-war period the three occupants of the ground floor rooms
were, significantly, Varley, Jack Beddington and Arpad Elfer. Edwards
recalled how the introverted Edward Bawden would arrive from the

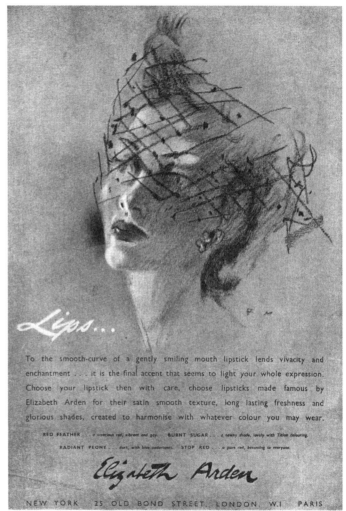

Opposite:
Advertisements for
Jaeger (left), 1937,
and 'Lips' (right) for
Elizabeth Arden, 1952;
both illustrated by
Francis Marshall

Right: Dahl Collings for
the International Wool
Secretariat, 1939

Far right: three small
advertisements for
Whipsnade Zoo

country, carrying his perfect artwork, absolutely overawed by the grandeur of it all, well out of his rural comfort zone.

Joan Bird, who had joined CPV in 1937, and who was to progress to become a group executive, in some reminiscences in the 1960s, provided a glimpse of the atmosphere of CPV in these early years –

'I'd come straight from school. Thought I'd joined a lunatic asylum – mind you after a month I'd found out what an exciting place it was. First I typed invoices, then I worked for Betty Prentis, then for an executive, then for Mr. Colman. I did print buying, made tea, ordered blocks, made tea, sun-bathed on the roof. Then I became an assistant on Jaeger and Elizabeth Arden…Terrific fun! So stimulating. The talent that passed through CPV has been fantastic. There was Paul Jennings on resistentialism – his own philosophy in answer to existentialism. Terence Prentis, a lovable genius with a

super collection of 5000 jazz records and 500 ties. There were the authors Peter Quenell and Gerard Tickell…'

One catches the fervor of it all – 'the sparkle and the hectic individualism of the early years' – and the fact that as a small band everybody mucked in – that opportunities were plentiful for those with the talent to advance, whatever their background or qualifications. Prentis's role was different to that he had had at Crawford's, for as art director he became altogether less hands-on, altogether more of a manager. Although an article in *Art & Industry* in 1938 gave examples of his work for Jaeger, Elizabeth Arden, the International Wool Secretariat and Whipsnade Zoo, he was quoted as being at one remove from the coalface –

'I don't do things myself because I can always think of someone else who can do them better; if you buy work from artists and photographers, then the whole world is at your disposal.'

Prentis's generosity as a manager is reflected in Joyce Booth's description of him –

> '[he] was one of those rare people who made you believe you were the only person capable of doing that particular job at that moment and you did it.'

Betty Prentis appears to have continued her work with Jaeger and to have been CPV's representative at the Jaeger Fashion Committee meetings. Although she and Terence divorced and each remarried in 1940, she continued to work at CPV and is listed as a director under her new married name Page (Tony Page had been a fellow artist at Crawford's). In a letter to *Art & Industry*, published just prior to the onset of the war, she wrote of her role as 'employing artists and designers as the director of an advertising agency', and as 'fashion advisor to large London stores.'

Although little is recorded of Varley's actual activities at CPV in this pre-war period, he is generally recognized as the business man of the trio (although that may not be saying all that much), providing a good deal of the energy and motivation needed in the early start up of a company. Of his management style there are mixed messages. All saw him as with considerable intelligence, with an instinctive talent for spotting talented people, and for an ability to inspire belief from a natural authority. His weaknesses have variously been described as once having taken on his bright talent, to demand a lot from them and to respond irritably if things didn't go his way. It was said of him that he picked the liveliest of minds and 'to have taxed them to their utmost.' Joyce Booth wrote of Varley as having a theory that friction often threw off sparks of creativity and added 'sparks did fly'. This has echoes of management theories of 'necessary conflict'. Roger Pemberton, a one-time creative director of the agency wrote of Varley –

Opposite: Arthur Varley on his wedding day to his first wife, Gwen Rhys Jones

Above: Varley, second from left, in Tunisia during World War II

'He was far from being a conventional capitalist businessman. The only point of money was to develop the agency's reputation, to live well and to indulge his extraordinary generous instincts.'

People remembered Varley's gifts of champagne when they were ill, and his wishing them good luck for various campaigns, albeit he could as well totally ignore them on the next meeting; and then there were the CPV celebrated parties! Yet it is not without its significance that Varley's large Rolls Royce, his generosity to himself, contained sleeping facilities for his chauffer-driven journeys down to his country retreat, rather than phones to further his business activities.

Whatever his strengths and weaknesses, and Pearson and Turner in their book *The Persuasion Industry* even suggest a touch of megalomania, Varley functioned as inspirational and as a magnet for aspiring advertising people – 'he is a shaman, a person who can arouse belief, and for those whom do believe in him, working for him has an excitement of its own.' The authors expand on this –

'For a copy-writer or an art man a spell at CPV is not an exericise in the techniques of applied merchandising. It is not the learning of a philosophy of selling and persuasion. It is a chance, quite simply, of working for Varley and being part of the unique, high-powered, nerve-wracking organization he has created around him.'

And, in spite of the necessary (or sometimes unnecessary) conflict, the young agency thrived. If one merely uses as a criterion the reputation of its artwork, CPV very soon began to be featured in *Modern Publicity*, the major journal at the time for assessing the best graphic design in any year. Year by year the number of CPV examples selected for the annual increased, until, in 1939, the agency overtook Crawford's, which until then had dominated the scene. CPV entries for that year included some half dozen advertisements Francis Marshall had illustrated for Jaeger, Elizabeth Arden and Gibson & Lumgair; a Shell-Mex & BP advertisement for Ethyl; four examples of posters for Barnes Pianos; and the first appearance of the names of Arped Elfer and Zoltan Glass, who were to become significant players for the agency in the post-war years. *Modern Publicity* of 1939 also included examples of CPV broadening its activities by dipping its toes into shop window display – for the Orient and for the Italian shipping lines.

And similarly, internationally, when *Gebrauchsgraphik*, the leading German journal on advertising art, devoted a complete issue to British advertising in 1937, although Crawford's hogged the pages,

Advertisement for W.H. Barnes Limited,
illustrated by Richard Linder, c1939

along with London Transport and Shell, of the handful of agencies given special mention CPV was allotted four pages – the first two devoted to Francis Marshall's work for Jaeger, the others including examples of work for Edinburgh Weavers and for Whipsnade Zoo.

At the start of the war, only some five years after its start-up, CPV had grown from a small band putting their hands to what ever came their way, to having a highly developed management structure with some ten specialized departments – marketing, creative, media planning, production, printing, display, editorial, promotion, export marketing, and advertising and promotion (of CPV). These were as listed in the agency's publicity, for in actuality *laissez fair* reigned – there were no sharp boundaries, no clear job descriptions; at best the organization could be described as creatively fluid, at worst, at times, chaotic.

An advertisement for CPV's services at the time listed over twenty clients, the majority being in the fashion and beauty industries, as to Jaeger, Elizabeth Arden and Norvic had been added Courtauld's (Viscana and Contessa), Cresta Silks, Dereta, Galeries Lafayette, Gossard Corsets, Goya Perfumes, the International Wool Secretariat, and the Women's Fashion Export Group of Great Britain.

But everything was put on hold with war looming. Both Prentises went into print, writing of their concerns for the future, particularly worried about the likely unemployment of artists if war was to come. Terence wrote passionately of artists' usefulness in society, demonstrating how he valued his profession as a commercial artist –

'We must do all we can to disabuse the official mind of a nation that artists are feckless, irresponsible, unbusinesslike creatures… They work longer hours and possess greater powers of concentration than the average civil servant.'

Advertisements for Edinburgh Weavers, 1937

Colman, Prentis and Varley self-advertisements, *Modern Publicity in War*, 1941

And Prentis' value system is portrayed in his urging as a slogan –

'Armaments may win the War. But it is the preservation of our peace-time cultural standards that will make the War worth winning.'

Betty promoted the cause of a women in commercial art who –

'...though trained to glorify and dramatise the looks of other women, she herself can afford to be no butterfly but must have learned the virtues of discipline and real hard work.'

Such opinions suggest the seriousness with which the Prentises viewed their vocation, and hints at the kind of atmosphere they must have tried to engender in the creative employees at CPV to take pride in what they all did for a living.

In the eventuality, it was Varley who immediately enlisted when war started, and the qualities he had shown in building CPV were soon to be recognized; having joined the Royal Army Ordnance Corps as a 2nd Lieutenant, he rose to the rank of Colonel. A history of the Corps describes Varley operating in wartime much as he had operated in CPV in its run up to the war –

'Colonel Varley – a civilian turned soldier – had a brilliant and unlimited restless energy. His speed of thought left lesser mortals standing, but there was nothing slap-dash in his planning and organization.'

Varley was named as one of three officers who had the credit for planning and executing the landing in North Africa of the First Army. He was twice mentioned in dispatches, and was awarded a CBE for his contribution, specifically for his, at the time, inventive idea of

A LITTLE LUXURY
YOU'VE EARNED . . .

Elizabeth Arden
SOAPS

F R E S H   F R A G R A N T   L A S T I N G

shipping military equipment in large crates, thereby anticipating the coming of the container industry.

Colman had also joined up, and with the two in the services, and other employees either called up or in other wartime employment, CPV was left in the hands of Terence (exempted from service with severe diabetes), Betty and a Miss Bird (described as the loyal and capable manager of accounts and administration). A self-advertisement put out by CPV, humorously pictured the situation with the copy –

> *'though some of our clients have moved… though some are in difficult places to contact…though some of our directors are in strange company… we of CPV are at your service.'*

Francis Marshall's elegant Elizabeth Arden women began to appear in uniform serving in the NAFFI, and his Jaeger women now had escorts in uniform or besported themselves in siren suits made popular by Churchill. CPV, as other agencies, rode the war out as best they could.

War-time advertisement for Elizabeth Arden, illustrated by Francis Marshall, 1941

CPV

are branching out in all directions

GETTING RE-ESTABLISHED

'**T**he war was over, everyone was bursting with enthusiasm. Some who had achieved high rank in the services reverted to their civilian positions and vice versa. It was mad and exciting and warm, lasting friendships were formed. There were difficulties too, paper was hard to come by, type founders had been bombed out and it was just too bad if there was not enough of the type specified to complete the job.'

… Joyce Booth caught something of the atmosphere at CPV at the end of the war – renewed motivation in spite of rationing and austerity.

During the war CPV had run on a skeleton staff. Varley, who is said to have turned down a peace-time army career as a major-general, returned to the fold. But his wartime experience, with its demands on his intelligence and ingenuity, had perhaps left him restless and even impatient with the day-to-day running of what was by then a well-rounded agency. He had a team of directors and a strong creative team, eager to flex its muscles. A description of his running a typical staff meeting possibly suggests that although he was prepared to go through the motions of consultative management, his mind was elsewhere –

'At staff meetings he would sit behind his large desk with a jug of fresh lemon juice within reach and chair discussions. Seated on the

fender would be those in the pecking order of the day. Decisions be made but rarely acted on. They would be out of date as soon as they were made, or so it seemed.'

Luckily for Varley there was a new battlefield and new battles to be fought, which would catch his enthusiasm and use his energy.

EXPORT

Britain was being geared up to revive its overseas trade, halted by the war, and to seek new overseas markets beyond the Empire. Varley was swept up in the competitive whirlwind that ensued. His foreign expansion plans for the agency were speeded up by the arrival of Jack Beddington as a CPV director, bringing the Shell account with him. Shell was developing its business, in 1950, into South America, into Venezuela in particular, and CPV on the back of this was to merge with a small local agency there to build one of the biggest agencies in that continent in the post-war years – Corporation Publicitaria Nacional (CORPA) with its own creative department and recording studios. A typed, but undated and unsigned note in one of the guard books at the History of Advertising Trust stated – 'Export advertising no longer an appendage to home turnover but an end in itself.' Another note caught the optimism and confidence of the time –

Opposite: Andre François, illustration for CPV self advertisement from *ARK* magazine

Right round the world
by British Airlines

You can get within striking distance of nearly every great city in the world by British Airlines. The European network converges on London—from London radiate fast routes to the five continents. At the controls are flyers famous throughout the world. Book to London by B.E.A.—thence to North America and the British Commonwealth by B.O.A.C. and to South America by B.S.A.A.

BEA · **BOAC** · **BSAA**

THE BRITISH AIRWAYS SYSTEM

British European Airways, advertisement, designed
by Arpad Elfer, illustrated by T. Barbosa, c.1948

'We have a staff with collective first-hand experience of advertising in all the major cultural areas of the world; a space-buying department capable of buying any media in any country; and a research and information section which keeps track of import regulations and basic marketing data and has contacts with Government Departments, Chambers of Commerce and so on.'

Added to this note were the names of Arpad Elfer, having experience and links to Berlin and Paris; John Hobson being an expert on Scandinavia, and Varley having the know-how on the United States. A guard book of 1947–8 shows CPV working overseas on behalf of its main clients with examples of advertising for Kolynos, Elizabeth Arden, Berkertex, BEA, Goya and the Hulton Press; in 1950, Advertiser's Weekly included an item of news that CPV was issuing a booklet 'First Steps in the American Market'; and in 1951, Varley hired Leslie Court, an ex-Reckitt & Colman executive, to lead CPV's Export Division.

The 1955 *CPViana*, the agency's in-house journal, celebrating the 21st birthday of the agency, had a special section devoted to CPV Export naming Leslie Court as its managing director, Geoffrey Robb as its creative director and Dimi Mangakis as the export manager. CPV Export seems to have operated in a variety of ways – having its own overseas offices, having merely representatives, and so on. The desire was to be represented in all the major markets but to be prudent about unnecessary overheads. A note, tucked into a guard book, suggested the use of small up-and-coming agencies in the countries to be targeted, or, possibly, independent consultants or 'a man of calibre'!

Undated, but probably in the early 1960s, CPV issued a booklet 'Marketing throughout the World', in which one page boasted –

'CPV – Colman, Prentis Varley…is an international advertising, marketing and public relations network, selling the goods and

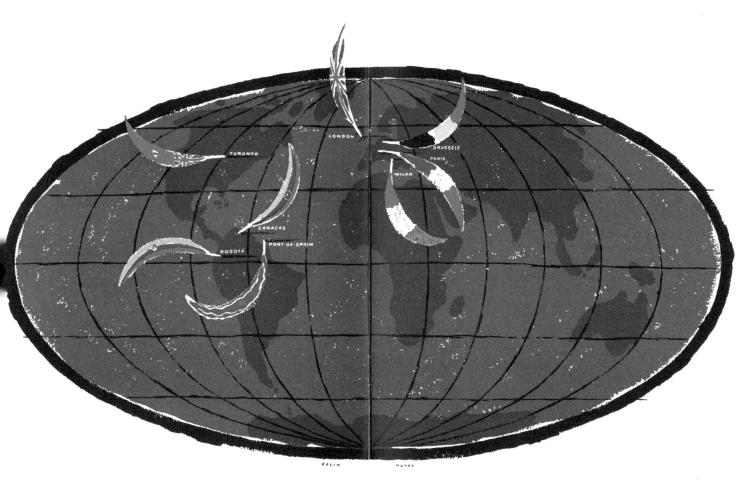

Illustration by Colin Mundy, for *CPViana*, 1955.

'The Young Nation' part of the 'Partners in Progress' campaign for Shell in Venezuela, photography by Arpad Elfer, produced by CORPA,

services of over one hundred and fifty clients in some seventy territories using more than twenty five languages.'

By the mid-1960s CPV had direct subsidiaries in some fifteen countries across Europe, the Americas and South East Asia. In *The Persuasion Industry* it was noted that by 1965 CPV was doing more overseas business than any other British agency. The Hon. Elizabeth Susan Douglas-Scott Montagu, who married Varley in 1962, wrote in her memoirs –

'Our 23 years together were as varied and fascinating as the Tales of Hoffman. As Chairman of an international organization, Varley's work took him all over the world, and as his partner I was to visit many of the places I had always longed to see: Scandinavia, Greece, South America and the United States. New York became a regular destination… Varley had a wonderful talent for bringing out the best in both places and people, and all our journeys were eventful. He even made Denmark seem exciting!'

A curious footnote to CPV's being quick off the mark in post-war overseas expansion is that it is said a minor motivation was that phones and phone lines (which were like gold-dust at the end of the war), were allocated, as priority, for companies complying with the government's concern to revive the export market.

Meanwhile, back at base, CPV's other directors, account executives, copywriters and artists were knuckling down to the daily grind, or, as many reported it, fun. Nevertheless, Varley himself would contribute to widening CPV's product base at home beyond fashion, and CPV began to become altogether more serious, recruiting fewer 'glamorous young chaps' and more people who had already proved themselves in business, as when it took on Brian Adam from Nestlé.

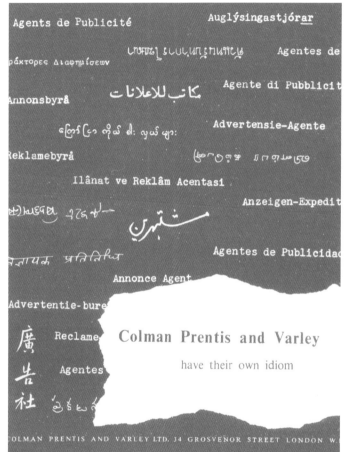

Colman, Prentis and Varley, self-advertisements

Quiz—masters dream of words to spell But the motorist only dreams of SHELL

— and when the days of "Pool petrol only" are over, you will find once more that — *you can be sure of Shell.*

JACK BEDDINGTON

Jack Beddington was, in some ways, a curious addition to the CPV Board in the post-war years. What motivated him to join CPV after the war is not clear. He had had a brilliant career at Shell, his name aligned with that of Frank Pick, at London Transport, as a major sponsor of artists for advertising and publicity in the inter-war years. And although working with greater restraints during the war as Director of the Film Division of the Ministry of Information, he nevertheless did much to further the cause of documentary film making and the careers of young film makers.

It is thought that he had been offered a general management position back at Shell but not at the level he expected. He was also said to have been offered the editorship of the Daily Telegraph — not as odd as it would seem, as he had no prior experience of advertising and publicity before tackling it at Shell and had done well with film from little first-hand knowledge. Whether CPV courted him in the anticipation of getting the Shell account and drawing on his considerable network, or he courted CPV, by 1946 he had resigned from Shell and joined CPV as its Vice-Chairman.

He quickly installed himself in Grosvenor Street, in a room resplendent in its furnishings and artwork. Joyce Booth wrote of the impression he made —

'Jack Beddington was a large oval man with an oval head; well-tailored and with a red lining to his jacket and a wide cumberband…..He sat in a room one would hesitate to call an office, with his back to the window, with original paintings that he had bought from up-and-coming artists in his days at Shell… He was an artist manqué, a shrewd operator with a sentimental streak.'

Each dog dreams
his favourite smell
But the motorist
only dreams of **SHELL**

—and when the days of "Pool petrol
only" are over, you will find once
more that—*you can be sure of Shell.*

The Psychiatrist dreams
(tho' he won't tell)
But the motorist
only dreams of **SHELL**

—and when the days of "Pool petrol
only" are over, you will find once
more that—*you can be sure of Shell.*

Platelayers dreams
run parallel
But the motorist
only dreams of **SHELL**

—and when the days of "Pool petrol
only" are over, you will find once
more that—*you can be sure of Shell.*

Opposite and above: Series of Shell advertisements, illustrated by Charles Mozley, directed by Margaret Sweeney, 1951

And Beddington did indeed bring the Shell account to CPV, but what else he did was not at all clear to the lesser mortals inhabiting the upper reaches of Grosvenor Street. *Art & Industry* in 1952 described him as responsible for Public Relations, and that may well have been part of his remit, for he was frequently to be seen with visitors who he took round the building, particularly popping in to the studio to show off whatever artwork was in progress.

But in addition to this, Beddington appears to have acted as a Human Relations Manager. He certainly was responsible for selecting some of the employees, as the copywriters Lilla Spicer and Ben Duncan and David Russell (later to be CPV's Chairman) have recorded. Others remembered discussing their salaries with him, along with other aspects of their employment conditions. And he seems to have had an interest in career development, setting up a training scheme, appointing an education officer, and encouraging new and established staff to take professional qualifications. He also appears to have tried to establish some kind of standards for CPV's independent-minded brood – being an early bird himself, he had a book placed at reception to be signed by late-comers (alongside the flowers he brought in from his garden)!

Amongst his other responsibilities Beddington, for a time, edited the CPV in-house journal – *CPViana*, a rather smartly produced publication compared to others of the genre – no sepia photographs of sports teams or summer company picnics – but well-designed in bright colours on good paper with articles and poems from employees, mostly in a rather satirical facetious style. Occasionally Beddington would contribute something himself, as when recording the death of his old friend Barnett Freedman, and when he got another old friend, John Betjeman, to write of their long-term friendship. In one edition of the journal Beddington

Cover for the 21st Birthday issue of CPViana, edited by Jack Beddington, 1955

fly **BEA** *to the snow*

Austria
France
Germany
Italy
Norway
Spain
Sweden
Switzerland

Advertisement for British European Airways,
photography and art direction by Arpad Elfer, 1958

described his job as 'removing personal difficulties and preventing unnecessary friction whilst the rest of the Board got on with the business of advertising.'

In spite of his successful role in relation to commissioning artists at Shell, Beddington seems to have had little influence on what went on in CPV's studio. However, in an article in *Modern Publicity* in 1949 he wrote how useful the journal was to advertising agencies as a source of potential artists, which perhaps suggests he was still on the lookout; he certainly brought in Abram Games to work on a series of posters CPV did for BEA/BOAC. Of course Beddington was into his 50s when he joined CPV, and by the late 1950s he began to work on a part-time basis, not only attending to his beloved garden, but contributing to a number of organisations relating to the Arts, including the Society of Industrial Artists, the Royal Society of Arts, and the Royal College of Art. He was still working at CPV when he died of a heart attack in 1959. It was Varley who read the lesson at Beddington's memorial service in St.Martins-in-the-Fields.

ARPAD ELFER

Terence Prentis died in 1946 and it is sometimes said that it was with undue haste that Arpad Elfer took up the crown. In his defence, he had already been at CPV some dozen years, and, becoming naturalized, he had served in the Pioneer Corps during the war, so by 1946 he was no doubt eager to develop his career.

Elfer adopted the title Creative Director for his new position at CPV, as he, for reasons not explained, disliked the word 'art'. In retrospect this was probably appropriate for him for he was certainly more of

Poster for British European Airways, designed by Abram Games, 1948

Poster for British European Airways, designed by Denis Bishop, illustration by Raymond Tooby, 1952

Poster for British European Airways, designed by John Hanna, 1954

Billboard advertisement for British European Airways, designed by Hans Unger, 1960s

Photography by Arpad Elfer
for *Lilliput*, January 1949

a total visualizer than someone particularly adept at applying pen or paint to paper, in spite of his art school training. His nephew, John Ross, described him as someone who quickly was able to 'encapsulate the mood, the style, and the desirability of a product'. Whatever else, Elfer was a realist. In a rare article by him, in *Art & Industry* in 1958, he stressed the importance of advertising artists being continually adaptable – that there were no rules to the game –

'He must put on a show on coarse newsprint multiplied a million times over by fast machines. He must be able to get the utmost glossiness out of full colour work on art paper in glossy magazines. He must create anything from new plastic package designs to mail order shots. He must be able to handle an idea on to the face of a 16-sheet poster so that it can be assimilated in a flash by the busy passer-by. He must know how to translate his message and his manner on to the television screen.'

As a manager Elfer had none of the sensitivity of Prentis. He had the energy and the inspiration to lead a creative team, but people had to do exactly as he told them (which was sometimes difficult with his convoluted English); and even when they did, they could still be found wanting. John Ross, who worked with his uncle as photographer, recalled that wherever Arpad had been he would have left behind him at least two earthquakes and a revolution. An anecdote in R.M.Carpenter's *Not Quite as Planned* tells of an executive going in fear and trembling to the Creative Director 'that awesome figure Arpad Elfer'. In his novel *The Agency Game*, Bernard Guttridge has a character, an art director, one Jon Zerglazz, which is a thinly, very thinly, disguised picture of Elfer –

'He was a very little man, though broad for his height. He had red curly hair, of an extraordinary colour, somehow more the colour of pink blotting paper than the natural tawny one expects of red-haired

Arpad Elfer in his photography studio

people. His eyes were small and quite black. His nose was stubbly. He wore a silver-grey suit. He had on a white nylon shirt, the sleeves of which came almost to his knuckles… Jon Zerglazz had come from Lithuania via Brussels, just before the war, and during and after the war had built himself a thoroughly deserved reputation for his ebullient advertising designs. All the artists I met at S.O.Q loathed and feared him.'

Foreign, Elfer certainly was, but from Hungary via Berlin and Paris, where he had worked for Crawford's; and he certainly was dictatorial with a degree of brusqueness and uncouthness in his style of operating. But, the reverse side of the coin, was that he brought to CPV an internationalism that they had lacked in the pre-war days, and an element of popular vulgarity (none of Ashley Havinden's puritanical modernism). Additionally, he took up and ran with photography, that was almost to replace original artwork for advertising design in the post-war years.

In Paris, the Crawford office was in the Vogue building and when working there Elfer was in touch with fashion and with fashion illustrators; and in London, he was part of a considerable network of European refugees. In no time CPV was making use of talents of the likes of René Bouché, a Czech, André François, a fellow Hungarian, René Gruau, from the Paris fashion world, and the photographer Zoltan Glass, also a Hungarian. Elfer established himself in a large house in Eldon Road, Kensington, which he furnished extravagantly with the likes of Russian gilded doors and 'antique' furniture from Bert Crowthers. Here he would entertain with lavish parties both for his considerable network of acquaintances and on behalf of CPV. The blurring of his own activities with those of his as an employee of CPV, possibly resulting in a conflict of interest, was particularly in evidence in the photographic studio, which occupied an extension

16 sheet poster by André François for Macdonald's Penguin chocolate biscuits, 1958

Jaeger advertisement (left); and colour illustrations for Elizabeth Arden
(right top and bottom); all illustrated by René Gruau

Left: D.H. Evans 'Christmas wise' railway hoardings poster, giant paper sculptures of bells made by Peter Hampton and photographed on the children, design and photography by Arpad Elfer, 1958

Below: poster for *Picture Post*, designed by Arpad Elfer

Opposite: poster for *Lilliput* magazine, photography and design by Elfer, 1950

at the back of the house. Originally CPV used Zoltan Glass for some of its photography but, as Elfer's enthusiasm for, and skill with the medium increased, he realized he could do much of the work more cheaply himself. And this became easier when Elfer's nephew, who was working with Glass, was filched, along with Glass's studio specialist John Donaldson. CPV's advertisements made an increasing use of photography and photographic models (for which both Elfer and Glass had a penchant), particularly in its work for D.H.Evans, BEA, Picture Post and Lilliput, Elfer doing much of the photographic work himself.

Although people found Elfer difficult, if not unpleasant, to work with, his influence pervaded the agency. Mary Gowing, herself a doyen of the advertising world, saw the positives in Elfer in her article devoted to him in *Art & Industry*, 1957. She knew him as demanding and shrewd, but additionally as 'witty, resilient, single-minded, prolific and tireless'. That Varley was intent on expanding CPV's overseas activities suited Elfer. At some stage he acquired the title International Art Director, and was soon to be found travelling widely with camera, both for his own and for CPV projects.

Ruth Gill (right) and the CPV team (below), from left to right, George Frost, Arthur Wilson, Colin Milwood, John Ross, Lilla Spicer and Arpad Elfer

CPV GROUP ART DIRECTORS, ARTISTS AND PHOTOGRAPHERS

As CPV grew in size, creative groups were formed under the umbrella responsibility of what came to be called the Creative Director – initially Prentis, then Elfer, and through, finally, to David Smith. The *Art & Industry* article on CPV in 1952, has it that there were seven 'art' groups, each carrying their own clients with whom they were encouraged to have direct contact. In the early years, after the war, there seems to have been a plethora of women group art directors, both responsible for their own teams, and contributing artwork themselves. The three names that occur most frequently at this time are Ruth Gill, Joyce Booth and Margaret Sweeney.

Ruth Gill trained at Chelsea School of Art where she was 'taught to see' by Henry Moore, and taught packaging design by the expert – Milner Gray. After a period as a freelancer, she joined the John Tait agency, eventually becoming its art director. The agency was small and with the need for all hands to the pump, Gill became something of an all-round advertising woman, rather than restricting her role to designing. Mary Gowing writing in praise of Gill said there was no aspect of an advertising campaign with which she did not become familiar. At CPV her main client was Fortnum & Mason, along with such others as Charnos and French of London. For Fortnums she was not only responsible for the work of the CPV artist Margaret Edwards, and the freelance artist Edward Bawden, but she did a good deal of the work herself, including devising the famous F&M logo. Ben Duncan, a copywriter, who worked for Gill on some of the Fortnum & Mason assignments wrote of her particular skill with typography –

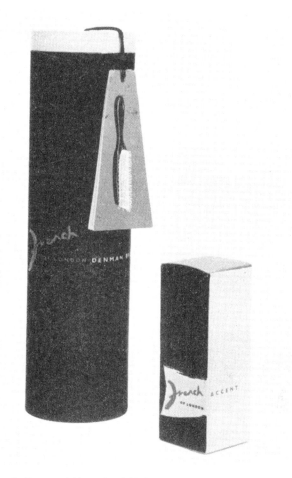

Designs for Fortnum & Mason (top left); silkscreen film poster illustrated by Harry Green for British Lion Films (bottom left); designs for French of London (right); all art directed by Ruth Gill

Far left: Advertisement for J&P Coats Limited, art directed by Joyce Booth

Left: Joyce Booth

'She treated the letters of the alphabet as design elements, turning them sideways or upside down or smear brushmarks across…

Although in appearance Gill was rather school-marmish, with glasses, plain hair style and simple folksy clothes, she was seen as a warm, compassionate team leader, smoking a cigar, and with a wicked sense of humour – focused, practical and straight speaking, both in running her team and in relating to her clients. She was to be poached from CPV by Mather & Crowther.

Joyce Booth also seems to have been a fun person, but with a sharp wit allied to an acute perceptiveness of people and their foibles. She is said to have been recruited into CPV by Prentis, having already had some experience at the Askew Young agency, and spending some time in the Women's Auxiliary Air Force during WWII.

Booth was to work with some of CPV's major clients, as Jaeger and Elizabeth Arden, as well as Dereta, Braemar, Ballantyne, Coats and Wedgwood. A record in one of a few of her guard books held at the History of Advertising Trust, has details of her handling, along with Cyrus Ducker and Roger Pemberton, a considerable campaign for the Gas Council, with a sizeable budget of close to a million pounds. A feisty woman herself, Booth, like other group directors, did not find working to Elfer particularly easy. A facetious comment

HIGH SPEED GAS
heat that obeys you

High Speed Gas—heat that obeys you

cosigas

Glorious gas heat – rooms warm faster!
Obedient gas heat – never any wasted! Heat when you want it.
Heat in a jiffy. Fireside cosiness and warmth on tap.
Faster, cleaner, easier, cosier – gas heats the world's most
comfortable homes! For one room warmth or central heating,
the quickest way is **HIGH SPEED GAS!**

HIGH-SPEED GAS IS NEWS—and so are all the latest HSG cooking
and heating appliances. Go see them at your Gas Showroom.

Long-running High Speed Gas campaign for the Gas Council,
'Cosigas' (left), 1960s, and billboard posters (above), 1965, art
direction by David Holmes, photography by John Donaldson

Advertisement for Deréta, illustrated by Francis Marshall, designed by Margaret Sweeney, c.1948

on their relationship in a CPV house journal describes Booth's dream social occasion as one where she has a glass of sherry in one hand and 'not to be called down to Arpad's room for a week'.

There are few records of Margaret Sweeney, who largely has to be known through her work. From this we know that she worked with Francis Marshall for the Dereta account, with Charles Mozley for the Shell account, with Geoffrey Salter for BEA, and with Cecil Beaton for what appears to have been a one-off advertisement for the Silk & Rayon Users' Association. That she was a designer of some repute beyond CPV, is exemplified by Sweeney being given the overall responsibility for the Womens Advertising Club of London's career book, which was illustrated by Ralph Steadman.

A male group art director who overlapped with these women, was Colin Millward, who in his career after leaving CPV came to be evaluated as one of the most influential creative figures in post-war advertising. Described as a rough Yorkshireman, born in Hull, Millward studied at both the Leeds College of Art and at the Ecole des Beaux-Arts in Paris, where he seems to have led a somewhat bohemian existence. However, needing to earn a living he initially joined Mather & Crowther before coming to CPV. He worked on a variety of CPV accounts including Jaeger, the Conservative Party, Findus, Amplex and Sunblest Bread. His secretary at the time, Judith Peppitt, remembers him using not only Francis Marshall and Andrew Robb, but the photographers Norman Parkinson and Anthony Armstrong Jones. 'Bill' Sherborne and Patrick Gierth, other CPV design executives, had served in the war, Sherborne in the Royal Air Force, and Gierth in the army before joining CPV, both men were to distinguish themselves at the agency before moving on to other advertising agencies.

Far left: Advertisement for the Silk and Rayon Users Association, illustrated by Cecil Beaton, designed by Arpad Elfer and Margaret Sweeney, 1951

Left: Advertisement for Regent Street, illustrated by Charles Mozley, designed by Margaret Sweeney, 1951

WOOL IS A BEAUTY TREATMENT IN ITSELF

"Wool moulds and flatters your figure like no other fabric."

THAT HIP PROBLEM! Of course, if your hips are perfect there's no problem at all—the moulding qualities of wool will show you off to perfection. If, however, your hips are a shade too wide do not wear a narrow skirt. Accentuate your waistline and break the width with pleats or soft folds so as to give fullness to your skirt. What could be more ideal for this than wool?

There is NO substitute for *Wool*

Issued by the International Wool Secretariat. F.1

Advertisement issued by the International Wool Secretariat, illustrated by René Gruau, 1947

Over the years, CPV used approaching one hundred artists, some fully employed by the agency, others freelance. What was, perhaps, characteristic of this pool was that a goodly proportion were 'foreign', many were emigres from Europe. These seem to have been drawn largely from Elfer's considerable network, such as his Hungarian friends André François and Zoltan Glass, and his friends from his Paris days – Rene Gruau and Rene Bouché.

The artist whose name occurs most frequently in relation to CPV accounts is Francis Marshall, one of the best known fashion illustrators of the time. After attending the Slade School of Fine Art and learning his craft with the Carlton Studios, he had built a name for himself, pre-war, illustrating for Vogue. But he broke his contract with them in 1937 when he began to work on CPV accounts, only having to put his career on hold when he served in Camouflage for the Royal Navy from 1939 to 1945. After the war Marshall's career broadened, for he not only worked for several advertising agencies but provided fashion drawing for the *Daily Mail* and wrote several books on illustration and fashion drawing as well as one illustrating the London scene. For CPV he provided work not only for Jaeger and Elizabeth Arden, but for Dereta, Goya and Odhams Press, and, curiously, for Fortnum & Mason's clothes, not a product for which they were best known.

In a diary note in 1964 he recorded –

'Very depressed. Sick of bad art directors who are neither artists nor do they direct, but, part pass on client instructions.'

Frustratingly, these inadequates are not mentioned by name, and one can only wonder that Marshall should have found any greater satisfaction providing illustrations for Barbara Cartland's books, which he did for the last twenty years of his life.

They call it *Breeze*

because it's country-fresh

It's the *new* soap in the news! Breeze brings you a thrilling all-over freshness, keeps the sparkle of Spring in your skin!

Mild rich-lathering Breeze, with its lasting country-side fragrance, keeps you cool-limbed and confident all the day long. From head to heels, from finger tip to finger tip — with Breeze you're fresh-air-fresh, fresh as an April shower.

For you, for him, for all the family — get cool green Breeze. *Price 6d. Bath size 11d.*

SPECIAL ANNOUNCEMENT
Breeze is the result of long research in the Crosfield Laboratories. Just as we are proud of the service PERSIL has given in millions of homes, so we believe that fresh green BREEZE with its invigorating lather and lasting fragrance is a toilet soap that will appeal to the whole family. This new product carries its guarantee of quality in the name of

Crosfields (CWG) LIMITED

Breeze!

and you're country-fresh from top to toe
BZI-1331-100

Above: René Gruau illustration for Dickins & Jones

Right: Advertisement for Breeze soap, illustrated by Francis Marshall, 1952

Far right: Film poster design for *The Red Shoes*, illustrated by Francis Marshall, art directed by Arpad Elfer, 1958

the Season in Regent Street

DICKINS AND JONES

Press advertisement for Dickins & Jones, illustrated by René Gruau, art directed by Arpad Elfer, c.1953

Gruau and Bouché only seem to have worked for CPV over relatively short periods, Gruau for Jaeger, Breeze, Dickins & Jones, Charnos, Goya and Elizabeth Arden; Bouché for Elizabeth Arden (he was said to be her favourite artist). Gruau would have been a catch as at the time he was working for the major fashion magazines and a number of *haute couture* fashion designers, particularly Dior. André François also appears to have only been commissioned for a short period, largely for CPV's advertising of itself and its services, a commission to which he brought his considerable talents as a quirky cartoonist.

Zoltan Glass, Elfer's close friend yet competitor, was to provide CPV with photography from just prior to the war, (when he did some work for Whipsnade Zoo), through the 1950s until Elfer began to take over where photography was involved. Glass had had a thriving career as a photojournalist in Berlin, specializing in car racing, before coming to England just prior to the war. He set up his own studio in London and became one of the most successful fashion and advertising photographers of the 50s with a particular interest in nude photography. He worked with Elfer for CPV advertising for *Picture Post*, *Lilliput* and D.H.Evans. His strength and originality lay in dramatic lighting, oblique angles and over-lapping multi-exposures.

COPYWRITERS

If one were to judge the value of any group to an organization by the part of the head office they occupied, CPV's copywriters would be placed above their artists being on the floor below. Yet, on the whole, CPV seems to have attracted more attention through its art

'*Someone* isn't using Amplex'
advertisement, designed by
Margaret Edwards, *c.*1956

and design than through its copy. This may have partly been because Elfer was said to have begrudged any words that he was obliged to accommodate into an advertisement! Copywriters would spoof him by saying that whatever the client or product, he would hand them a drawing with the comment 'Write three vitty words'! Generally copywriters seem to have touched down at CPV for relatively short periods of time, and then gone on to make their reputations in entirely different fields, as with Paul Jennings, Peter Quennell and Ben Duncan. Of course there were exceptional commissions that stimulated CPV's copywriters to originality that caught the nation's interest, for example the General Election campaign of 1959 –

*'Life's better with the Conservatives
Don't let Labour ruin it.'*

and on a more humble subject –

'*Someone isn't using amplex*'

But more usually CPV's copywriters tended to the more prosaic, as for BEA – 'Come to Britain', for Norvic Shoes – 'You buy them for style, you wear them for comfort', for Scotts Porage Oats – 'simple as ABC to make, supreme in flavour', for Goya – 'the loveliest thing about you…', and much much more at a similar level.

CPV's slogan for Conservative Central Office, for the General Election, possibly gave the agency more exposure than any other of their projects. It was a particularly crucial election as Eden had just resigned over Suez and all three parties had new leaders. At the time Geoffrey Tucker was working at CPV and as he had stood (unsuccessfully) as a Tory candidate, he was naturally assigned the job. The original idea for a slogan had come from Lord Hailsham, but Tucker, and his colleague, Ronald Simms, made it more snappy, turning

COLMAN PRENTIS AND VARLEY LTD

Advertising

. . . we like to cater for all tastes . . .

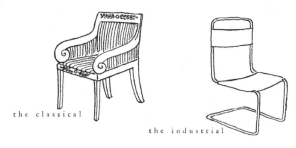

the classical

the industrial

the fashionable

the gay

at

34, GROSVENOR STREET,
W.1.

Telephone . . . . *Mayfair 9111*

Above: Colman, Prentis and Varley,
self-advertisements, 1947

Right: Shell full page
advertisement in *Lilliput*, 1950

you can't trust arithmetic

7,200,000 people between 14 and 23

who have never heard of SHELL ?

Never heard of SHELL —

the name on the red and green petrol lorries,

on the petrol pumps, on the famous posters ?

Nonsense !

Yet that's what our statistician thinks.

People start noticing advertisements at 14, he says,

and with an 800,000 average annual birthrate

that means that $9 \times 800,000$ people

have become 14 since 1939.

7,200,000 don't know about

SHELL's country-wide distribution network

SHELL's three great British refineries

SHELL's research

SHELL's 80% of our wartime refining (lubricants)

SHELL's tanker fleet (the world's largest)

SHELL's oilfields earning foreign exchange

for Britain

7,200,000 !

But surely veterans will have told them

you can be sure of SHELL

As a matter of fact

Hulton Research is primarily concerned with press readership. Its main study, the annual Readership Survey, breaks down the readerships of some ninty-six publications, by class, sex, age-group and region; and again by special interests and social habits, such as car-ownership and cinema-going. Additional studies have covered, for example, the rural market, several retail trades, the beer, wine and spirit market, and smoking. Specialised work of this kind produces valuable ' by product '

information about social and economic habits in this country. Much of this information, together with the resources and experience of Hulton Research is available, without fee, to advertisers and agents with advertising and marketing problems. Hulton Research provides the basic facts about the advertising public, the solid factual background against which professional judgment may best be exercised. Hulton Research will continue to offer its contributions to advertisement planning in 1950.

HULTON RESEARCH

Hulton Press Ltd., 43-44 Shoe Lane, London, E.C.4.   CENTRAL 7400.

instagas

Full flame heat at the flick of a wrist!
That's the miracle of instant gas. Heat you can see,
heat that obeys you, only comes with clean, quick gas. Meals come faster,
homes are warmer, brighter lives are lived by gas! Only heat
that's right for today—the instant heat of **HIGH SPEED GAS!**

soupagas

Food's ready quickly—thanks to gas!
Just flick a wrist for full flame heat.
Cooking's perfect—thanks to gas! Control things exactly: gas obeys you.
See what you're doing without
temperature guesswork. Food's ready faster,
food tastes better, everyone's happier with **HIGH SPEED GAS!**

Far left: Advertisement for Hulton Press Limited, Patrick Gierth

Left: 'Instagas' and right, 'Soupagas', advertisements for The Gas Council, illustrated by Siné (top) and Manzi (Bottom), c1962

'Life's Better with the
Conservatives' poster, 1959

'Things are better under the Conservatives' into 'Life's better with the Conservatives', and adding 'Don't let Labour ruin it'. The campaign can said to have been validated by the Tories increasing their number of seats (albeit the votes they attracted actually dropped). Varley was to claim that CPV was not a Tory slanted organization, that the election job was merely a commission; but certainly there was a Tory bias to some of the directors (including Beddington), and it is thought that some clients were deterred by this.

CPV was again to the fore on behalf of the Conservatives for the election following the public relations crisis of the Profumo affair. Such had been the success of the previous slogan that it was felt it could not be bettered, and CPV decided to turn to visuals using documentary film illustrating how well the Tories had performed whilst in power (supplied by an out-of-house freelancer – Roger Hardy).

Another example of a coup by CPV copywriters was when they revolutionized the image of gas for the Gas Council, cold-heartedly ejecting the long-serving and much loved Mr. Therm. Roger Pemberton, who had joined CPV to be in charge of copy, having learnt his trade at J. Walter Thompson and the London Press Exchange, recalled how they played around, coining new adjectives, to give gas the image of cleanliness, safety, and, above all, speed, as 'whizzy gas' and other such whimsy.

Tucker, who had trained as a copywriter before joining CPV, wrote, whilst there in 1950, of the skill of a copywriter –

'Copywriting is only enjoyable in fact, when there is excitement in the air; when you are trying to sell two packets of a product when only one was sold before; when you are writing freshly and convincingly; when you are deeply involved and interested in an account; when new problems and

new ideas are continually turning up. None of these things happened at my first agency; they do happen now and thank goodness for it.'

Denis Hodson, another CPV copywriter described his fellow copywriters facetiously, yet affectionately, in the 21st birthday issue of its in-house journal –

> 'The copywriters are as keen as mustard. Smart intelligent people with a good grasp of modern marketing conditions, they never use a word too many or too few, and, of course, they are very nice people.'

The CPV copywriter, a part-timer, who was possibly to be the longest stayer, and certainly one who was much admired by her colleagues and clients, was Lilla Spicer. Spicer, born Lilla Gibson-Taylor in 1915, had had a vague inclination towards becoming a journalist on leaving school, and, as was the custom for girls at the time, took a course as a shorthand typist. She started work at a magazine – *The Cabinet Maker* on an old typewriter with letters steeped down either side; and found it boring!

When only eighteen she managed to get a job as a secretary to *Vogue's* Social Editor who tended to be picky as to which jobs he was prepared to do, resulting in Spicer grabbing at the opportunity she was looking for. He would say to her – 'you go; you can write it all down', and go and write she did. On one such job, to cover the Czechoslovakian spas, she met her future husband. When her boss was transferred to the Paris office, Spicer was promoted to Assistant Sub-Editor. But with staff leaving to enlist for the war Lilla found herself doing three editorial jobs, including Beauty Editor, and, conveniently becoming pregnant, she left. Even when she returned for a time, she couldn't work out a suitable balance of home and family, and reluctantly she left. Advised of a vacancy at CPV by

Lilla Spicer at *Vogue* (right), and at CPV (below)

Fortnum & Mason
Valentine's day card,
copywriting by Lilla Spicer,
illustration by Edward
Bawden, 1950s

Anne Scott-Jones, she was able to negotiate with Beddington a more suitable time commitment at CPV.

Spicer's strengths for CPV were her quick wittedness and whimsical humour, so particular beloved by the British. Whether writing copy for D.H.Evans, Jaeger, Dickins & Jones, Telemac or Fortnum & Mason, a cute little jingle would immediately come to her mind, reminiscent of much of the outpouring from the Stuarts advertising agency in the inter-war years. Perhaps because of this Spicer tended to be used only on 'prestige' accounts and not those requiring hard selling. One example of her work was a jolly little book for Jaeger, with illustrations of some of the animals whose coats provided the material for Jaeger clothes. A typical Spicer piece to accompany an illustration of an angora goat was –

'Angora goats have curly coats
quite different from the rabbit;
mohair's the stuff, so soft yet tough
it seems like magic – grab it.'

and similarly for the cashmere –

'The Cashmere goat, aloof, remote,
is apt to be elusive…
he little knows how far that goes
to making him exclusive.'

Spicer's triumphs were, perhaps, with her work for Fortnum & Mason, in particular for its Xmas catalogues, for which she is said to have thought up most of the ideas as well as writing the copy. For these she was working to Ruth Gill, as group art director and with Edward Bawden, who provided the iconic illustrations. One of the

*A*ngora goats
    have curly coats
        quite different from the rabbit;

mohair's the stuff,
    so soft yet tough
        it seems like magic – grab it.

Jaeger use mohair to conjure up their toughest travel coats, their laciest shawls

*A*ngora Goats

'Angora goats' from the *Jaeger Natural History* book, produced in a limited edition of 200 in 1953, illustrations by Jean Hugo and copywriting by Lilla Spicer

most successful of these was for Xmas … for which Spicer punned *CATalogue.* Ben Duncan wrote of the hilarious times he and Spicer had brain storming around the theme of 'cats'; he described her as a 'magical phrase-maker'. For the section on F&M's catering service in the 'Cat' issue, she provided some popular whimsical doggerel of the time –

No human demand could be greater than that
of a pedigree, pampered, fastidious cat;
we bear this in mind when clients insist
on fabulous feats at the drop of a list.

We conjure up parties in no time at all,
no banquet too large, no luncheon too small.
Experienced staff are prepared for the strain…
Call us, and relax, when you next entertain.

When her copy editor, John Pearce, left in 1960, to be followed by the departure of Elfer, a personal friend as well as a work colleague, Spicer began to lose motivation and left as well. She died in 2007, at the ripe old age of 91.

green Breeze gives you! With its light, freshening fragrance, it's a fine soap, family soap,  the soap they all love using...

Real chlorophyll—nature's own ingredient that makes the countryside so green— goes into cool green Breeze

CPV CLIENTS

Eyes clear, provocative, amused. Eyes veiled with thought, mysterious, impenetrable. Eyes transparent as the Mediterranean on a summer day. All the life of the face is in the eyes. They are the first feature to show fatigue from overwork or too much gaiety, strain from wind and weather, the bitter hint of coming age. They must be cared for always and never more so than these first days of winter-into-spring.

★ Begin and end your day by bathing the eyes with Miss Arden's *Special Eye Lotion*. It cleans, strengthens, soothes . . . 4/6 and 10/6 ★ *Venetian Special Eye Cream*. It nourishes the delicate tissues and muscles around the eyes. Pat it on gently and leave it on all morning, 6/-. ★ For puffy eyes, use Miss Arden's *Puffy-Eye Strap* over *Special Astringent* pads. Afterwards apply *Velva Cream*, 4/6. *Special Astringent*, 9/6. *Puffy-Eye Strap*, 14/6. ★ To lengthen and strengthen the eyelashes use *Venetian Eyelash Grower*, 8/6. ★ For make-up, use *Venetian Eyelash Cosmetique* and vary the shades according to your mood and costume. Black, brown, light & dark blue, green or violet. 5/8. ★ To enhance the colour of the eyes use *Ardena Eye Sha-do*, again in varying colours—In fifteen shades, 4/6

Elizabeth Arden

25 OLD BOND STREET LONDON WEST ON1

Opposite: Advertisement for Breeze Soap (detail), 1953

Above: Advertisement, 'eyes', for Elizabeth Arden, illustration by Francis Marshall, c.1937

'BEAUTY' ADVERTISEMENTS

From the start CPV advertising very much focused on women consumers, with beauty to the fore, its two main clients in the area being Elizabeth Arden and Goya.

Varley, himself, had brought in the Elizabeth Arden account, and a good number of advertisements for the company in the years running up to the war, illustrated by Francis Marshall, were considered of sufficient merit to be included in the annual *Modern Publicity*. Elizabeth Arden, herself, very much the grande dame, was considered difficult to handle and to need extra special attention. Although in command from across the Atlantic, CPV staff were said to feel her influence as if she were in the next office. She actually had a London-based go-between for her advertising, one Mary Wichello, who had been her secretary and was devoted to her. CPV staff were so in awe of Mary's pernicketiness over detail that they would rehearse their meetings with her in advance. Elizabeth Arden had to approve everything and there is an account of someone having to fly in haste to Gruau's studio in the South of France for him to change a hair style on one of his drawings which madame had disliked.

There are a number of 'folk tales' of CPV personnel encounters with Elizabeth Arden in New York, as when the young Lord Montagu, accompanied by his ceremonial robes, visited her in the year of the

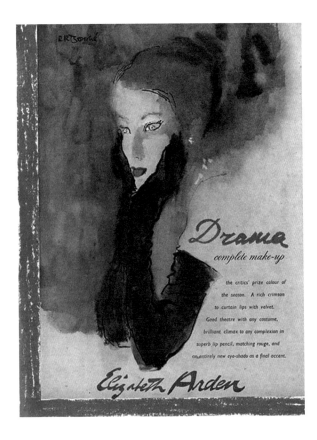

Advertisement for Elizabeth Arden,
illustrated by René Bouché, 1950s

Coronation (the robes were for a speaking tour he was doing). At the time Montagu was working for CPV's 'Voice & Vision'. Arden claimed he promised her tickets for the Coronation, which he later denied. Whatever, she did come over for the event, and she remarked to Varley how thoughtful he had been to send her flowers to her hotel in her racing colours (which may have just been coincidental but gave him brownie points). Varley was to continue to take an interest in the account, for which his charm did much to ease things along.

A less happy outcome was when Elfer suddenly decided to take a firmer grip on artwork for the Elizabeth Arden advertisements which, during the war had largely been sent over from New York, CPV merely anglicising the copy. Elfer took Francis Marshall with him to visit her in New York, along with sketches and copy of 'matchless prose' provided by Peter Quenell, the layouts done by Joyce Booth. Elfer's extraordinary out-sized ego had under-rated that of the diva, in particular he had not appreciated the rivalry between her and Helena Rubinstein, which led her to have anti-semitic tendencies which spread to include Elfer. Having his fingers burnt, Elfer retreated, swearing to have nothing more to do with the account and leaving it in the hands of Joan Bird, the account executive, who seems to have been able to establish a better relationship.

Both Francis Marshall and Gruau were to illustrate CPV's Elizabeth Arden advertisements, art directed in the post-war years by Joyce Booth. Rene Bouché's name also occurs for the account, a Czech émigré to the United States who became madame's favourite illustrator. Looking back on her work for the account Joyce Booth wrote wryly –

'Her (Elizabeth Arden) era has gone with the pink and white complexion, blue satin and pink chiffon negligees… She believed in her products and her staff believed in them too.'

The pink and blue Elizabeth Arden had preferred meant Booth having a constant battle with the printers to attain the exact shades specified.

Working with Goya appears to have been an altogether less stressful affair; handled more closely by Elfer along with Joyce Booth, and then by Robert Sherborne. Francis Marshall and Gruau were again used for the account, but also the English illustrator Charles Mozley, not usually remembered for work of this sort.

The illustrations for CPV's 'beauty' accounts provided by Marshall, Bouché, Gruau and Mozley, each caught a different aspect of feminity.

Three advertisements for Goya; illustrated by Charles Mozley, and designed by Derek Riley (left), illustrated by René Gruau and designed by Robert Sherborne, c1955 (middle), and for *Vogue*, 1953 (right)

Advertisement for French of London, designed by Margaret Edwards, 1960s

Gruau's signature style was, perhaps, the most easily recognizable and the most sexy. He could just use eyes, or a gloved hand, a nape of a neck or a shoulder, by which to express the utmost sensuality, made more so by his strident use of black, white and red; Marshall's women could be said to be attractive rather than alluring; whilst Bouché and Mozley appear to be nearer to Gruau, but altogether less strident.

An example of CPV's use of photography for 'beauty' accounts, was its work for French of London, who claimed to be the first hairdresser to run advertising campaigns. Margaret Edwards worked with Ruth Gill on this account, along with Joan Bird, who had got the commission and was its account executive. For once Elfer's Eldon Road studio was not used, CPV turning to a freelance photographer, John Cole. French, himself, took an active part in the development of the advertising – Margaret Edwards described him drawing his name, to be used across the advertisements, with a bit of wood dipped in paint. She reported how easy it was to work as a junior both with Joan Bird and Ruth Gill, with a constant easy flow of ideas, no-one pulling rank. The space buyer would give them the dimensions and placing for an advertisement, sometimes a challenge for its narrowness, and Edwards and Gill would receive perhaps up to thirty or forty contact prints Cole had taken of the model in his studio. They would make their selection from these in perfect harmony, and then Edwards would proceed with the lay-out, being allowed a certain leeway, as when she slipped a silhouette of French himself into one advertisement.

And then there was Breeze! Pearson & Turner in *The Persuasion Industry* devote some four pages to CPV's Breeze campaign signifying its impact at the time. The Americans were already frank in their advertisements for deodorants, whilst the British had been

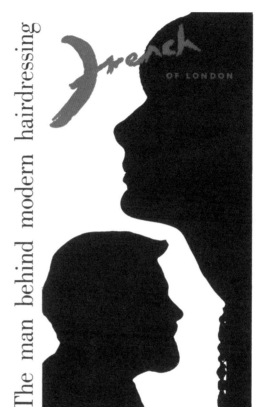

Advertisement designed by Margaret Edwards and Ruth Gill for French of London, with the silhouette of French himself used for the smaller figure, 1960s

I'm quite happy with New Breeze thank you very much.

ANDREW CHRISTIANSEN
Kirkwood Creative Group.

Breeze soap advertisement, designed by Ronald Kirkwood and Sue Perry, 1962

altogether more coy. CPV had already had the Breeze soap account for Unilever, when it was placed in the hands of Ronald Kirkwood, the agency's young television director. He wrote –

> 'The post-war girl wasn't the wilting romantic young thing of the pre-war ads and she was much too sophisticated for the overtones of haystacks and apple cheeks…'

Kirkwood went for the sensual rather than the sexy, and using the top fashion photographer, Henry Clarke, CPV astonished the public with what has been rated the first major advertising campaign to show images of a naked model. Sue Perry, along with Kirkwood, wrote the copy, a typical example being –

> 'Darling, it's no use being coy about perspiration problems. The fact is (any doctor will tell you) you're perspiring all the time; and it's perfectly natural.'

FASHION ADVERTISEMENTS

CPV was to work for a number of women's fashion companies, including Dereta, Horrockses, Berketex and Norvic, but Jaeger was its major client in the industry. It was largely on the strength of having the Jaeger account that the Prentis's had left Crawfords, and it stayed with CPV for a number of years. In the pre-war years Jaeger still held on to its link with Dr. Jaeger's theory of the healthiness of wearing animal based materials. There are examples of Betty Prentis's work in the pre-war years, certainly from 1930 onwards, one, curiously, advertising a woolly bathing costume – 'the nearest possible feeling to being in your birthday suit'.

check - its

JAEGER

Jaeger advertisement, illustrated by Walter Grieder

CPV was to help convert the image of Jaeger from 'all about health' to 'all about fashion', largely aided by the splendid illustrations provided by Francis Marshall and, for a short time from 1953 to 1957, by Gruau. Marshall had worked with the Prentises for Jaeger from before the war. An undated letter of that period from Marshall to his wife tells of a job he is doing with Mrs. Prentis who is about to set up her own agency. By 1937, Marshall had left Vogue, for which he had worked from 1928, and was working for a number of agencies including CPV. He has a diary entry of providing nine small drawings for Jaeger for 'standard' adult clothes. Although Marshall was to work on a number of other CPV's accounts it is for his brilliant illustrations for Jaeger that he is, perhaps, best remembered.

Jaeger was keen to change its image in the post-war years from being rather worthy and reliable and CPV came up with the slogan 'The Fashion Name for Wool'. Although Elfer's name is connected with Jaeger in the 1950s, Joyce Booth seems to have shouldered much of the work and certainly recalls working on the lettering —

> 'I was allowed to add the straw lettering to the full page ads. It took a lot of nerve to make those brush strokes.'

Although the characteristic Jaeger logo of the time is usually ascribed to Elfer, some references mention Betty Prentis, whilst the Jaeger archive even ascribes it to Marshall himself. By 1952 *Art & Industry* were full of praise for CPV's contribution to the transformation of the Jaeger image —

> 'With a beautifully designed product to start with, a first-rate fashion artist like Francis Marshall and copywriters who understood the meaning of brevity and kept to the point, the advertising was immediately in character with the product to be sold and resulted in considerable market expansion...'

Advertisement for Deréta, designed by Arpad Elfer,
illustrated by Francis Marshall, c.1951

Advertisement for Horrockses, c.1953

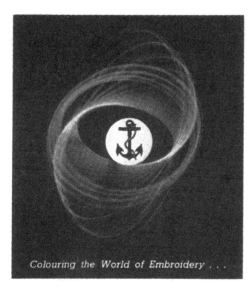

Advertisements for Darley Mills Company Limited, designed by Patrick Gierth, c.1949

Advertisement for Coats, designed by S. John Woods, c.1954

Advertisement for Anchor, designed by R. Sherbourne, photography by G. Gilbert, 1956

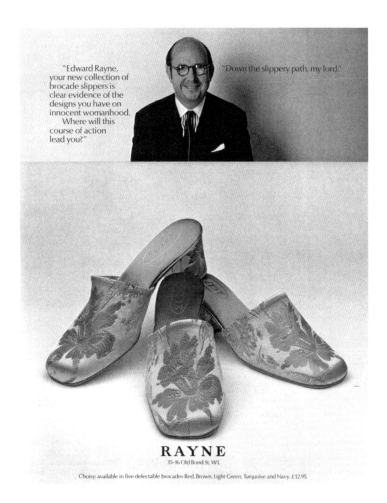

"Edward Rayne, your new collection of brocade slippers is clear evidence of the designs you have on innocent womanhood. Where will this course of action lead you?"

"Down the slippery path, my lord."

RAYNE
15-16 Old Bond St, W1.

Choisy: available in five delectable brocades Red, Brown, Light Green, Turquoise and Navy. £12.95.

Rayne shoes advertisement featuring Edward Rayne

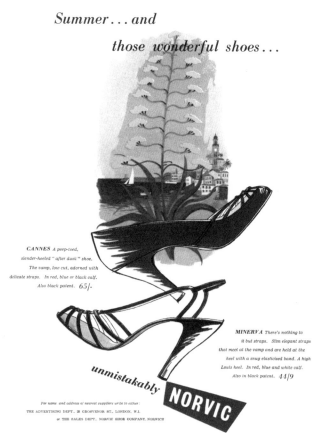

Summer . . . and

those wonderful shoes . . .

CANNES *A peep-toed, slender-heeled "after dusk" shoe. The vamp, low cut, adorned with delicate straps. In red, blue or black calf. Also black patent.* 65/-

MINERVA *There's nothing to it but straps. Slim elegant straps that meet at the vamp and are held at the heel with a snug elasticised band. A high Louis heel. In red, blue and white calf. Also in black patent.* 44/9

unmistakably **NORVIC**

For name and address of nearest suppliers write to either :
THE ADVERTISING DEPT., 28 GROSVENOR ST., LONDON, W.1.
or THE SALES DEPT., NORVIC SHOE COMPANY, NORWICH

Advertisement for Norvic Shoe Comapny, 1953

Advertisement for Courtaulds, illustrations by Francis Marshall, 1941

Advertisement for Berkertex 'summer collection', illustrated by Geoffrey Salter, art directed by George Frost, 1954

Although Marshall's and Gruau's illustrations can sometimes be confused, they usually initialled their work, and each took a slightly different slant – Gruau presented the Jaeger woman as sophisticated, and if he provided a background to his figures it would tend to have in it a luxury car or a plane; Marshall, on the other hand, still made his women classy, but tended more to the casual or country look, sometimes including a whole family plus dog, sometimes a marquee suggesting some event in a country house.

Elfer had the curious idea of producing something of special note for Jaeger, a booklet, which has been referred to in relation to Lilla Spicer – *Jaeger's Natural History* – with cute drawings of animals from which wool was derived, provided by Jean Hugo. It was issued in a limited edition of two hundred and printed by Cowell's of Ipswich. It took a considerable time to produce, and by the time it came out it had lost something of its prestige value as Jaeger was, by then, starting to use man-made fibres. Nevertheless it is worth noting that Hugo was a rarity in that he expressed how much he enjoyed working with Elfer!

DEPARTMENT STORES

D.H.Evans, like so many London department stores, had started as a small shop on Oxford Street, but by WWII it had extended to some one hundred and forty feet of frontage. And, like other

'Fashion wise' advertisement for D.H. Evans,
illustrated by Ruth Sheradski, designed by Arpad Elfer

stores, it was to suffer from wartime bombing, and to face the post-war years needing a new look, both in its building and in its image. The actual building escaped structional damage but new, striking interiors were designed for it by Stefan Buzas, yet another Hungarian émigré.

After the war, the store decided to focus on women and children's fashion, but particularly to target middle income 18 to 25 year olds. CPV was brought in in 1946, with Elfer leading the team, Lilla Spicer working on the copy and George Frost the graphics, although, over time, through to the 60s, others were involved, including Edward Wright, Joan Jordan, Barbosa, Geoffrey Salter and Joyce Booth. An illustrator and fashion artist, Ruth Sheradski, who was later to find fame running her shop 'Loot', so influential on 1960s fashion, was also to be used for the D.H.Evans account.

Elfer had thought to bring in Glass for the photography, but decided it would be more economical if he did most of it himself. It was the slogans that were decided upon that set the tone for CPV's D.H Evan's advertisements – 'Fashion Wise' and 'Shopping Wise'. Certainly these met Elfer's demands for brevity of copy. Although Spicer generally worked with Elfer on the campaign, it is thought that it was Barbara Baddeley who came up with these two word tags.

It is said that it was Spicer who discovered, when she was in a hairdressers, the model initially used; and soon Zoe Newton's face, along with the dragged brush 'Fashion Wise', was to be seen all over London Underground, until she was poached by Crawford's for their milk campaign. Other models followed, to be taxed by Elfer, as one who had to balance precariously under a headdress of lighted candles constructed by Joyce Booth. In addition to photography and photo-montage, Elfer used drawings, cut-outs and even small scale

'Christmas wise' posters for D.H. Evans,
designed by Arthur Barbosa (above), 1946,
and designed by Edward Wright (right)

Left: 'Needle wise' advertisement for D.H.Evans, illustrated by Edward Wright

Above, right and below: three 'Fashion wise' advertisements for D.H. Evans, design and photography by Arpad Elfer

Above: Advertisements for Dickins & Jones, designed by
Arpad Elfer, photography by Zoltan Glass

Right: Design for Fortnum & Mason by Margaret Edwards

models in his work for D.H.Evans. *Modern Publicity* considered his efforts sufficiently good to be featured in its annuals throughout the 40s and 50s and into the 60s. Mary Gowing wrote of Elfer's D.H.Evans advertisements and posters –

> 'This advertising has the breath of life in it. It glows. It is gay, spontaneous, exciting and friendly.'

Fortnum & Mason, similarly, in the post-war years, decided they needed to refresh their image, and brought in CPV to replace Stuarts as their advertising agency. Nevertheless CPV seems to have been infected with a certain amount of the Stuarts agency's whimsy, that had been so popular with Fortnum & Masons customers in the pre-war years.

The store's account was very much Ruth Gill's baby, albeit Elfer seems, very occasionally, to have been on the scene. Gill collected round her a goodly team of artists, photographers and copywriters, Margaret Edwards describing the constant flow of ideas within the team, which meant that sometimes no single person could claim the idea for a particular job.

Gill, however, not only directed the team, but herself originated the 'F' and 'M' logo that was to appear in a variety of forms on all the stores advertising and packaging. Peyton Skipwith described Gill's typography as 'clean', and cleanly it appeared not only with the logo but on all the company's invoices, stationary and other paper-work.

Lilla Spicer was Gill's main copywriter for the store; her artists Edward Bawden (when humour was required) along with Margaret Edwards, Ronald Fern and Francis Marshall, amongst others. Fun was the word – and Margaret Edwards, junior artist and go-between on the account, and Ben Duncan, both remember with pleasure the hustle and

Present day living — present day giving

Appropriate presents for veteran car fans. Waste paper bin, 42/6.
Round trays, 12 in. size, 50s., 14 in., 54/6.
Table mats, 18/6 each. Platter mat, 25/6.
Also available : 1 pint Brierley crystal beer tankard
engraved with vintage car designs — £2.16.0.
Royal Worcester jumbo cup and saucer, vintage car design, 43/9.
Square glass ashtrays, 10/6 each.

Fortnum & Mason Ltd., 181 Piccadilly, London, W.1. Regent 8040

Advertisement for Fortnum & Mason, art directed by Margaret Edwards and Ruth Gill

Fortnum & Mason 250th anniversary Christmas catalogue, designed by Edward Bawden, 1957

Fortnum & Mason for the essential and the exceptional

An elephant never forgets to stop
at the Maharajah's favourite shop,
if you have any special whim
you only have to follow *him*

Fortnum & Mason Ltd. 181 Piccadilly, London, W.1
Regent 8040

Fortnum's stands on the corner of Piccadilly
and Duke Street, St. James's. It is a very special shop
as you will soon see when you step inside.
Where else do you find frock-coated gentlemen,
the most civil of servants, taking grocery orders
by telephone—or even telepathy, if it is *that* type
of customer? And isn't it surprising to find
the floor above entirely devoted to women's clothes
of the most admirable kind?
Further up, you find men's clothes:
further down, luggage and gifts;
in between, there's a Soda Fountain,
a Spanish Bar and a Travel Patio.
On top of everything, there is
first-rate hairdressing (for women).

Fortnum & Mason Ltd. 181 Piccadilly W.1   Regent 8040

Fortnum & Mason press advertisements, illustrated by Edward Bawden, copywriting by Lilla Spicer

bustle and laughter it involved and the exceptional standard achieved as when a press advertisement for the stationary department won a Layton Award (the long forgotten, but then prestigious, award for creativity in advertising).

Bawden had been inherited from Stuarts, and was considered a real asset, not only because of his excellent drawing, matching Spicer's whimsy, but for his outstanding organization – without any fuss and on time he would arrive at Grosvenor Street with his separations in perfect order, albeit his prescence there seemed rather incongruous – a rural-like figure, terrified at the splendour. Francis Marshall, although better known for his CPV assignments for Jaeger and Elizabeth Arden, did a number of illustrations for Fortnum's catalogues and advertising. His diary recorded some half dozen occasions, between 1954 and '59, when he was needed for fashion drawing of blouses, dresses, suits and the like.

But it is for the Fortnum's catalogues, especially the Christmas ones, that CPV is best remembered, Lilla Spicer frequently conceiving the themes (as described previously), and Gill with overall responsibility. Mary Gowing, in her article in *Art & Industry*, praised Gill for the wonderful colour combinations used – 'the exciting juxtaposition of blue greens and green blues, combinations placing considerable demands on the printers.' Peyton Skipwith, was likewise full of praise for Gill's sparkling work with Bawden –

> '…the most truly classic image created by this pair of perfectionists is the 1957-8 advertisement for caviar and foie-gras, with Bawden's whimsical sturgeon and duck contrasted with Gill's clean-cut 'F' and 'M' on their respective tin and jar.'

Possibly of all CPV's advertising work the ephemera remaining from the Fortnum & Mason account is most fondly remembered and is certainly the most sort after by collectors, although few such could name the agency involved.

THE PRESS

The Hulton Press had been founded by Edward Hulton in 1937. It mainly published magazines and, along with the likes of *Farmers Weekly*, it published some of the most popular of the time – *The Leader, Lilliput* and *Picture Post*, the latter selling, in the 1940s, nearly two million copies per week.

Elfer, along with his 'friend' Zoltan Glass, was to work on the advertising for both *Lilliput* and *Picture Post*. For *Lilliput*, the pair not only provided posters for the underground bearing distorted faces, a wheeze thought up by Elfer carrying such tags as 'Such a Nice Change, Lilliput', but wrote stories with such cute titles as, in 1948, 'Two Ways of Shooting Politicians'.

For *Picture Post*, again Elfer was to direct the artwork and Glass to provide the photographs. For many of these advertisements the image was dominant (so much to Elfer's liking), with copy limited to a few words as 'Britain's Best'. Ben Duncan recalled the toughness of the *Picture Post* staff when, on one occasion the CPV copywriter was taken ill, and he had to prepare the copy in haste ready for the dummy – 'Now write it boy and make it sing!' Many of the tags CPV thought up for *Picture Post* reflected the stark honesty of much of its contents, as 'calls a spade a spade', and 'lets the cat out of the bag'.

One of CPV's most brash, but effective, contributions to Hulton Press publicity was for its comic *The Eagle* which the vicar

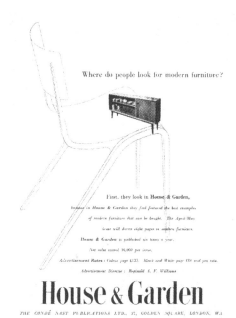

Above: Advertisement for *House & Garden*, designed by Margret Sweeney

Right: Advertisement for *Housewife*, designed by Arpad Elfer

Advertisement for the *Eagle* comic

Advertisement for *Picture Post*

Poster for *Picture Post*, photography by Arpad Elfer and Zoltan Glass, 1950

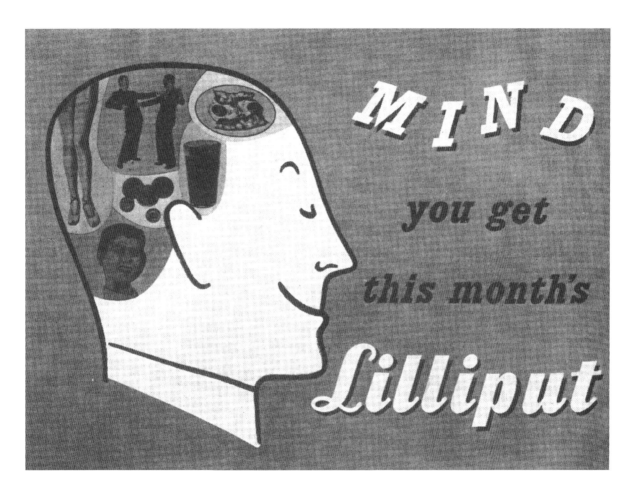

Poster for *Liliput* magazine, art directed by Arpad Elfer, 1950

Right: Coupon folder cover, circulated to newsagents for the *Eagle* comic launch, 1952

Far right: a Humber Hawk with a mounted plastic eagle, used to advertise the first issue of *Eagle*, 1950

Opposite: Shell-Mex and B.P. Limited poster, Festival of Britain 1951, designed by Barnett Freedman.

Marcus Morris had sold to Hulton, unable to launch it satisfactorily himself. For this the young Lord Montagu, working at the time with CPV's public relations subsidiary Voice and Vision, got himself involved, and, somewhat recklessly, was given his head. Enormous plastic eagles were mounted on cars and driven across England to launch the first issue of *The Eagle* in April 1950. Reckless or not, some 900,000 copies were sold. And it was Voice and Vision that later on was involved in organizing the Hulton Achievement Awards prize-givings.

CPV was also to do some work for Condé Nast, both for *House & Garden* and for *Vogue*. This appears largely to have been managed by Margaret Sweeney, using the illustrator Eric on occasions, but more frequently the advertisements were attributed to her alone.

SHELL

Although CPV seems to have done some work for Shell prior to WWII (there is an example of an advertisement for Ethyl dated 1939), it was Beddington who brought with him the Shell account when he joined CPV in 1946. Petrol had been one of the first products to be rationed when the war started and by 1942 petrol for private motoring was withdrawn and only available for war-related activities; it did not come off rationing until 1950. During the war the petrol companies were 'pooled' together and CPV was to make much of this when in the run-up to derationing it alerted consumers to the event of Shell products again becoming readily available. CPV picked up the 'ditty' style of copy writing that had been so typical of Shell's inter-war press advertisements –

Many an owner talks all
day about his Vauxhall.
His pride will be unendurable
When SHELL is procurable.

and

The pool fan dreams of a winning spell
But the motorist only dreams of Shell.

and Barnett Freedman's red and yellow poster for the Festival of Britain bearing –

Lets be gay
Good-bye to sorrow
POOL today
But SHELL tomorrow.

CPV's work for Shell in the early 1950s appears to have been handled largely by Margaret Sweeney, sometimes credited just to her, at other times as using other artists including Peter Ray, Charles Mozley, and Steve Jennings. In the late 50s Patrick Gierth and Colin Millward began to direct Shell's artwork, the artists they employed included John Hanna, David Janes and André François.

As already noted, it was the Shell account that proved so useful to CPV expanding into South America, and this provided opportunities for the travel-loving Elfer to provide photography for some of the account's advertisements. A joint training course was set up by which it was hoped CPV got a better understanding of Shell's place in the oil industry whilst the Shell employees picked up at least a rudimentary appreciation of what was involved in advertising.

Shell poster, originally in red, yellow and black, design and photography by Arpad Elfer, 1958

fill up and **feel the difference**

dreaming
of
shell

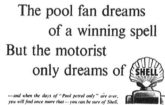

The pool fan dreams
of a winning spell
But the motorist
only dreams of SHELL

—and when the days of "Pool petrol only" are over,
you will find once more that — you can be sure of Shell.

Press advertisements for Shell-Mex and B.P. Limted, 1950s

CPV can certainly be accredited with putting Shell's name back in the public's eye when individually named brands gradually reappeared in the 1950s, but by the early 1960s the Shell account was to go to Ogilvy & Mather and then to Mather & Crowther.

PUBLIC RELATIONS

Voice and Vision was set up as CPV's public relations arm. Run by the likes of John Metcalf and Sydney Wynne, it grew into one of the biggest firms in its sector in London. Metcalf had come from the

Above: Shell Italy, J. Blackall, 1954

Right: direct mail advertisement for Shell-Mex and B.P. Limited, designed by Margaret Sweeney, 1952

BBC and Wynne had been a leader-writer with the *Daily Herald*, so both were bringing a wider expertise to the pre-war stretch of CPV personnel. Initially Voice and Vision were handling mainly CPV clients, but the percentage was gradually reduced, until eventually Voice and Vision had its own client list (perhaps only overlapping some twenty percent with those of CPV), and virtually functioned independently of its parent company. At its height it was said to have had some fifty personnel handling some sixty clients.

It began to bring in 'names', and particularly took on a number of established military figures, as Major General Shortt, who had previously been the public relations officer for the War Office. These appointments were useful in bringing gravitas to Voice and Vision, but, more essentially, for their influential social networks, both in and out of government.

Such contacts proved particularly useful for Voice and Visions' overseas work, as with the handling of the account for Rhodesia, for which parties of members of parliament were enticed out to the Federation, and much lobbying went on in the Houses of Parliament. The unit worked for a number of other African countries, and got a certain amount of press coverage in its efforts to transport Gibraltar, in the eyes of the public, from 'apes and sieges' to being an attractive holiday destination. Wynne, with an affected modesty, declared of Voice and Visions' successes —

'…we are not hidden persuaders. We are just a bit better than the chaps next door in the field of communication.

Left: An early cartoon of Lord Montagu, c.1951

87

LEDGER Copyright	1. DATE	2. NARRATIVE	3. REF.	DEBIT DETAIL £ d.	DEBIT TOTALS £ s. d.	CREDIT DETAILS £ s. d.	CREDIT TOTALS £ s. d.
	24 7	Gas Council	✓	4860 7 –	2 10 7		
	"	C.C.O.		15509 5 6	6 0		
	"	Fortnum & Mason		2 0 2½	31256 4 6		
	26	Susan Small		0 1 2	740 0 8		
	28	Manns		125780 – 4	6430 6 0		
	2 8	Sunblest	✓	24 6 3	24		
	"	Austin	✓	700			
	3	Norvic		54			

G.K. HASKINS
"THE FIDDLER"

THE FINALE

An advertising agency's capital lies not so much in what it physically owns, as, in the case of CPV, property in Mayfair, but in its employees and its client list. By the early 1960s CPV had the fourth biggest billings in the United Kingdom, lying behind J.Walter Thompson, the London Press Exchange and S.H.Benson's; with its public relations subsidiary, Voice & Vision one of the largest in its field. In *The Powers of Persuasion*, Varley is congratulated having –

> '… built one of the top five agencies from a standing start, particularly through war-fractured years, was a substantial feat. At the same time put together a robust international organization ahead of other agencies…'

But CPV's capital, at least part of it, was on its way out, one way or another. Although Beddington may not have been a key player in the early post-war years, he had added to the agency's classiness, aided its overseas expansion, and lent to it his considerable influential network. By the mid-1950s he was spending altogether more time in his beloved garden than in Grosvenor Street, and he died of a heart attack in 1959.

CPV's overseas activities did much to stimulate Elfer's interests in foreign parts, and his adoption as International Creative Director

Opposite: Leaving card for G.K. Haskins, the company accountant, on his retirement

validated his wanderings abroad. But these, in turn, led him to further exploit his photographic talents and, possibly, to divert his focus somewhat from the more routine jobs back at base. In any case, by the mid-60s he was reaching retirement age and he was to leave by 1968 to 'do his own thing'. Although, over the years, his creative team had not found him easy to work with, he had been inspirational, and, for one, Lilla Spicer found she lost interest when he was no longer around.

And what of Varley himself; born at the beginning of the century he too was reaching the age at which others would want to slow the pace, and he, too, had a garden to tempt him. Pearson & Turner described Varley as they saw him in 1965 –

> '…an amiable, slightly portly, good-looking Old Wykehamist, with a pipe and a tweed suit – rather a comfortable man these days, who has recently taken to silver-rimmed pince-nez for reading and who often prefers talking about his garden than his business.'

And it is possible that his fourth marriage, to Elizabeth Montagu, may have offered new horizons. She was a woman of some substance herself, with a range of talents that had led her into the theatre and into film and eventually into setting up a small commercial film company that had actually done work for CPV, as for its client Ryvita. But in her memoires she declared that this work had led her to hate

Right: Colonel Arthur Varley, known to everyone as 'Varley', and Elizabeth Montagu on their wedding day, 1962

Far right: Jack Beddington in his beloved garden

'all those "ad men" in their sharp suits and the superficiality of it all.' Varley seems to have been the exception! And his overseas expansion may have eventually lost its excitement – even the initial stimulation of understanding the necessary adaptations of advertising for each new culture could, after the first dozen, become routine.

Whilst CPV was becoming an important force in international advertising it was somewhat in decline at home, with accounts such as BEA and Shell moving to other agencies. Varley, himself, began to realize that the expense of his overseas ambitions was having an adverse effect on his home-based bread and butter. Even

with apparent success of CPV's overseas 'empire' there was a lack of control, particularly financial, the whole enterprise sometimes being referred to as a 'folie de grandeur'. Additionally, Varley was to admit that he never quite cracked the really big clients as J.Walter Thompson had with General Motors and Erwin Wasey with General Foods. He had never interested himself much in the day-to-day financial administration of his agency, putting such matters in the hands of 'lesser mortals', albeit he was said to have been able to 'read' a set of figures remarkably quickly to get the gist of what was going on. As it turned out, it is possible he should have given the detail rather more attention. J.Walter Thompson once declared –

'I distrust brilliance and anybody to whom the word can be applied; thoroughness is what I swore by.'

Unfortunately for CPV, Varley had more of the former than the latter, his brilliance being his intellect. It was said of him that 'he brought intellectual glamour even to the most mundane'. Intellectual ability and social charm are, however, rarely sufficient for commercial success, without steely determination and focus.

And Varley's skill at 'picking the liveliest minds and taxing them to the utmost' meant that although he gathered round him an elite talent he knew little about the actual grooming of them; although his demanding and 'taxing' could be stimulating, a necessary conflict for action and achievement, Varley's stubbornness and impatience meant that he lost some key players, who might otherwise have proved to have been successful inheritors of the crown.

Roger Pemberton wrote of Varley –

'He liked to be the grit in the creative oyster and, I suspect, enjoyed a bit of anarchy in the process. This meant that CPV was a somewhat fissile structure that made possible the various breakaways which stole the golden eggs in the shape of clients and talent that he had laid.'

In the advertising industry there was always a natural movement of personnel from agency to agency, and sometimes back again, done without too much rancor – it was to be expected. Few agency's had the stability of personnel as had Crawford with Ashley Havinden and the Sangster sisters. At CPV, there were the usual comings and going, but then there were bigger rifts, as when, as early as 1955, John Hobson, who had been assistant managing director, left after

a difference of opinion with Varley who opted for the Pepsi-Cola account in competition to Hobson's Sunfresh (it was not considered respectable practice for an agency to handle competitors, yet most did). Hobson not only took accounts with him, as Cadbury's, but some key personnel, as Pat Gierth, a promising creative director. Similarly John Pearce, who had been brought in from *Picture Post*, on his departure to set up what became Collett, Dickenson and Pearce, took clients, including Harvey's, and personnel, including Colin Millward and, the clever public relations man Geoffrey Tucker, who had had a major hand in CPV's work for the Conservatives for the 1959 election, Another key player who was to have a major disagreement with Varley and leave, was John Metcalf, who had done well with Voice & Vision. And even the loyal long-serving David Russell fell out with Varley over the suggestion of mergers, and was to leave and set up his own agency. Several of these would have been competent heirs to Varley. John Hobson & Partners, and Collett, Dickenson, Pearce & Partners were in fact, to become major players in the industry, ending up near the top of the league. Varley could be said to have been careless of his heritage.

Varley was to have a number of offers from other agencies to buy CPV. In his empire building he had already formed an association with a large American agency – Kenyon & Eckhardt, and it was they who, by 1973, had gained financial control of CPV. They, in turn, were to merge with French Gold Abbott to become Abbott Gold Kenyon & Eckhardt (presumably all having egos to ensure their names were kept in a not very snappy title). The names of Colman, Prentis and Varley were gone forever from the enterprise they had started with such optimism some thirty years before. Varley, who died in 1985, had his name honoured, however, with the establishment of the Varley Memorial Award, most suitably for work in the field of communications, at the Royal College of Art in 1988.

APPENDIX I

CPV CLIENTS

Amplex
Austin Motors
Ballantyne
Barnes Pianos
BEA/BOAC
Bentalls
Berketex
Gibson & Lumgair
Glengarry
Goddard's
Gossard
Goya
Greaves & Thomas
Harvey's
Horrockses

Hulton Press
Innoxa
Braemer
British Lion Films
British Steel Scaffolding
Cadbury's
Charnos
Coats Cotton
Colas Emulsion
Condé Nast
Conservative
    Central Office
Courtauld
Crème Simon
Crosfield's

Curran
du Maurier
Darley Mills
Deréta
Dickins & Jones
D.H. Evans
Ealing Studios
Elizabeth Arden
Fortnum & Mason
French of London
Galeries Lafayette
General Steam
    Navigation Co.
International Wool
    Secretariat

Italian Lines
Jaeger
Kolynos
Lustron
Macdonalds
Mann's Brown Ale
Norvic Shoes
Orient Line
Pedigree
Pepsi-Cola
J.Arthur Rank
Regent Street
    Association
Rembrandt
Ryvita

Sanford's
Scott's Porrage Oats
The Gas Council
Silk & Rayon Users'
    Association
Shell-Mex
Unilever
Wedgwood
Yardley

APPENDIX II

SOME ARTISTS EMPLOYED OR COMMISSIONED BY CPV

L.R.Allston
Andre Anstrutz
Aufseeser (Hans Tisdall)
John Bainbridge
Barbosa
Michael Bartlett
Edward Bawden
Cecil Beaton (one-off)
Tim Bell
Denis Beytagh
Denis Bishop
J. Blackall
Joyce Booth
René Bouché
J. Brooks
David Caplan

Hugh Casson (one-off)
John Castle
Christel
Dahl Collings
Coverley
Djurkovic
David Edgell
Margaret Edwards
Gwen Eickler
Arpad Elfer
Eric (Carl Erikson)
R. Ferns
Jonathan Foss
André François
Barnett Freedman
T.L. Frost

Patrick Gierth
Ruth Gill
Zoltan Glass
Henry Green
Walter Grieder
René Gruau
John Hanna
James Hart
David Holmes
David James
Cyril Jeffreys
Steve Jennings
Joan Jordan
David Judd
Angela Landes
Richard Lidner

Manzi
Francis Marshall
Colin Millward
George Morris
Charles Mozley
Frank Munn
Rosemary Palmer
Betty Prentis
Terence Prentis
Peter Ray
Derek Riley
Rothholtz
G. Salter
Hans Schleger
Ruth Sheraski
R. Sherborne

Siné
David Sisman
David Smith
Eric Stemp
Margaret Sweeney
Ann Swyer
Raymond Tooby
Jean Varda
Paul Walter
Jack Whitsett
S. John Woods
Edward Wright

APPENDIX III

BIBLIOGRAPHY

1938 'Creative Men of the Agencies – No.4 Terence Prentis', *Art & Industry* vol.25

1952 'Advertising that Advertises: Colman, Prentis & Varley Ltd', *Art & Industry* vol.52-53

1954 Bernard Gutteridge, *The Agency Game*, Weidenfeld & Nicolson

1957 Mary Gowing, 'The Creative Mind in Advertising – Arpad Elfer', *Art & Industry*

1957 Mary Gowing, 'The Creative Mind in Advertising – Ruth Gill', *Art & Industry* vol.63

1965 John Pearson & Graham Turner, *The Persuasion Industry*, Eyre & Spottiswoode

1977 Philip Kleinman, *Advertising Inside Out*

2003 ed. Ralph Montagu, *The Honourable Rebel: the memoirs of Elizabeth Montagu*

2005 Ben Duncan, *The Same Language*, Faber & Faber

2006 Ruth Artmonsky, *Jack Beddington, the footnote man*, Artmonsky Arts

2012 Ruth Artmonsky, *Designing Women*, Artmonsky Arts

Have you heard...

that C.P.V are always happy

to see people

with talent.